For Elizabeth and all members of our families

A DICKENS DINNER

A Dinner Theatre Play

By

MARIAN STROZIER

Copyright © 2017 Marian Strozier
All rights reserved.
ISBN: 978-1-7365054-0-3

The cost of one play/script copy should be far less than publishers normally charge for performance royalties. The play, however, is fully protected from copyrights. No part of this work may be reproduced, stored in a retrieval system or transmitted in any form by any means, electronic, mechanical, photocopying, recording or otherwise, without permission of the publisher.

A catalog record for this book is available from the Library of Congress.

Cover Design: SelfPubBookCovers.com/BravoCovers

Contents

INTRODUCTION vii

CAST OF CHARACTERS xi

ACT I 13

ACT II 19

ACT III 31

INTRODUCTION

On December 1, 1985, *A Dickens Dinner* made its debut performance to a packed house at a restaurant in Saginaw, Michigan. The objective of the performance was to raise funds for the St. Vincent Home in Saginaw, a service provided by Holy Cross Children's Services.

That agency was founded in 1948 as Boysville of Michigan, but its St. Vincent Home had actually been in existence for over 75 years. In 1875, the St. Vincent Orphan Home opened in a three-room dwelling that provided 15 orphaned children with a home and education.

That was just five years after the death of writer Charles Dickens and some 30 years after the 1843 publication of Dickens *A Christmas Carol*. Dickens's novella was so packed with inspiration and memorable characters, that even today, the mere mention of its name immediately conjures up the harsh but loving lives of Tiny Tim's family in 19th century London.

The title also brings to mind the forced transformation of a jaded old bachelor into a kind, grandfatherly figure who claims to be "as merry as a schoolboy," after discovering the joy of being given a second chance to mend the miserly mistakes made during the latter years of his existence.

The overarching lesson--as Saint/Pope John Paul II's biographer George Weigel observed, is that "The deep truth about humanity is that when we make our lives into a gift for others, as life itself is to each of us, we come into human fulfillment."

Today, Holy Cross Children's Services claims to be one of the largest private, not-for-profit providers of child services in Michigan.

As one of the many who labored on that cold Michigan night, producing *A Dickens Dinner*—to bring a bit of comfort to the lives of those children--it is my hope there will be many future performances of this dinner theatre play that will likewise bear fruit for benevolent causes.

In the meantime, in the words of Tiny Tim, "May God bless us, every *one!*"

Peace and all good,

Marian Strozier
April 7, 2017

CAST OF CHARACTERS

MUSICIANS: (Will play intermittently throughout performance)

COURT HERALDS: (One for every three tables)

QUEEN VICTORIA (One)

QUEEN'S COURTIERS (Lords, Ladies in Waiting, etc.) (Three to Five)

GHOSTS OF CHRISTMAS PAST (One for every three tables)

GHOSTS OF CHRISTMAS PRESENT (One for every three tables)

TINY TIMS (One for every three tables)

EBENEZER SCROOGE(S) (At least one. Preferably one for every three tables)

GHOSTS OF CHRISTMAS YET TO COME (One for every three tables)

MAGICIANS (One or more)

JUGGLERS (One or more)

CAST OF CHARACTERS
(Continued)

PUPPETEERS   (One or more)

MIMES   (One or more)

STILT-WALKERS   (One or more)

BALLERINA   (One or more)

**STRINGED
INSTRUMENT MUSICIANS**   (One or more)

RIBBON DANCERS   (One or more)

**PRESENTERS OF
THE FOOD
SCULLERY**   (One for each table)

SERVANTS   (One for each table)

ACT I

Scene 1

Setting: We are in a stylish Victorian banquet hall as it might appear during the lifetime of playwright Charles Dickens. The tables are set with tablecloths, flowers, dinner plates, cutlery. (For each guest: two forks, one knife, one spoon) and glasses (two per guest: one for water and one for cider or another drink).

(The COURT HERALDS enter the room. They each stand in front of the center table of a group of three tables. As they speak, they will address the audience seated at all three tables. This method will be the same for all GHOSTS, TINY TIMS and SCROOGE characters.)

COURT HERALDS (loudly in unison)

All rise and bow or curtsy to your queen!

(Instrumental Song: "GOD SAVE THE QUEEN"")

(HERALDS exit. QUEEN VICTORIA enters, walking gracefully past each table, nodding as her subjects bow or curtsy to her. A group of courtiers follows her. When she is finished with her promenade, she and her courtiers take their places at center stage where all can see.)

QUEEN VICTORIA:

My Lords and Ladies, we welcome you to this dinner in honor of the admired and much respected Mr. Dickens, whose writings, plays and performances I have much enjoyed. I hope you take pleasure in this meal and we wish you all a most happy Christmas. Good night.

(The queen and her courtiers exit.)

Act I, Scene 2

(The GHOSTS OF CHRISTMAS PRESENT enter the room, also standing in front of the center of three tables. As they enter, they are singing in unison, accompanied by musicians, a verse from the song, "WE WISH YOU A MERRY CHRISTMAS.")

GHOSTS OF CHRISTMAS PRESENT

**(Singing to
"We Wish You a Merry Christmas"song)**

We wish you a merry Christmas,
We wish you a merry Christmas,
We wish you a merry Christmas,
And a happy new year!

(Pause, then speaking in unison)

In Christmas fashion we presume,
To feed and entertain you.
But if you scorn our Christmas cheer,
Old Scrooge's ghosts may *pain* you.

(The GHOSTS OF CHRISTMAS PRESENT exit while singing, a verse from the song, "DECK THE HALLS," accompanied by musicians.)

GHOSTS OF CHRISTMAS PAST

(Singing to "Deck the Halls" song)

Deck the halls with boughs of holly,
Fa-la-la-la-la, la-la-la-la

'Tis the season to be jolly
Fa-la-la-la-la, la-la-la-la

Don we now our gay apparel
Fa-la-la, la-la-la, la-la-la.

Troll the ancient Yuletide carol
Fa-la-la-la-la, la-la-la-la.

Act I, Scene 3

(The PRESENTERS OF THE FOOD enter as the ghosts exit. There is one PRESENTER for each table. Each one is carrying a carafe of wine and/or cider.)

PRESENTERS OF THE FOOD

We have within our vessels
Fair drink to quench your thirst,
For some it may be much too strong
And so we ask that first,

You choose from one among you
A brave one who will taste,
To rule out any poison,
While we depart... in haste!

(The PRESENTERS OF THE FOOD quickly but carefully place their carafes on the tables and hurriedly scramble toward the exit, as though leaving to avoid bodily harm.)

BRIEF INTERMISSION WHILE DRINKS ARE POURED

(MUSICIANS play a happy holiday song)

ACT II

Scene 1

(EBENEZER SCROOGE(S) enter(s), frowning, grumbling and pacing.)

EBENEZER SCROOGE(s)

Are you a "Scrooge?"
Well, I should know,
For Christmas made me FROWN!"
Are *you* the one,

(SCROOGE(S) points a finger at a member of the audience)

Who says, "HUMBUG!"
When others aren't around?

Well, if you are,
I hope you'll change.

(SCROOGE(S) first shake their heads as though they cannot believe what they're saying. Then, they slowly begin to smile, broadly.)

Yes, that's my Christmas wish.
You all know WHY,
And with that thought,
I'll introduce your fish.

(SCROOGE(S) exit, singing the opening verse from the song ""God Rest You Merry, Gentlemen," accompanied by musicians")

EBENEZER SCROOGE(s)
(Singing to "God Rest You Merry," is an English traditional Christmas carol)

God rest you, merry gentlemen,
Let nothing you dismay,
Remember Christ our Saviour
Was born on Christmas-day
To save poor souls from Satan's power,
When we had gone astray.
O...tidings of comfort and joy
Comfort and joy,
O...tidings of comfort and joy

Act II, Scene 2

(PRESENTERS OF THE FOOD enter, each carrying a platter of some type of cooked fish and sauce. This will be served family style, one platter per table. This same presentation style applies to all food; one large serving dish per table.)

PRESENTERS OF THE FOOD

We are the servers of the fish,
And also of the dish,
For first must come the dish you see,
Before there comes the fish.

And now, we must request of you,
A keeper of the dish,
Who then will pass the plates around,
On which there is... the fish!

(PRESENTERS OF THE FOOD exit)

BRIEF INTERMISSION WHILE FISH COURSE IS SERVED AND EATEN

(MUSICIANS play a happy holiday song)

(When all have been served from the fish platter, the "SCULLERY SERVANTS" appear to remove the platters and carafes. If any food remains on the platters or liquid remains in the carafes, they can ask, using a Cockney accent, *"Can I finish this up for ya, loves?"* At that point, they can place the remainder of the food on the plates of those who want it and pour all remaining liquid into the glasses of those who wish for more. They then remove carafes. This signals the next scene of the performance. Backstage—in the food staging area—the carafes will be refilled for use in Scene 4.)

Act II, Scene 3

(GHOSTS OF CHRISTMAS PRESENT enter, taking their places, each at the center of three tables.)

GHOSTS OF CHRISTMAS PRESENT

Old Scrooge, he hated Christmas.
And much to my bemusement.
But my-----he CHANGED!
And in his name,
We offer this amusement!

(The company of entertainers enters. They are possibly MAGICIANS, JUGGLERS, PUPPETEERS, MIMES, STILT-WALKERS, BALLERINAS, STRINGED INSTRUMENT PLAYERS, RIBBON DANCERS, ETC., who briefly perform at each table and exit after one turn around the room.

These are short performances.

For example, one card trick at a table. A STRINGED INSTRUMENT MUSICIAN might perform only one song while strolling around the room. The STILT-WALKER might exit after walking past all tables. The overall performance is flexible, but should be choreographed.)

Act II, Scene 4

(As the last of the company of entertainers recently exit, the TINY TIMS enter, again taking their positions at the center of each of their three tables.)

TINY TIMS

My name is Tiny Tim, you see,
And it was my poor plight,
Which helped old Ebenezer,
When he finally saw the light.

But first, he had to see the *Ghost*,
The one that makes us *shiver!*
He'll be here soon, but first, we'll have
Some turkey without liver!

(TINY TIMS exit, followed by the entrance of the PRESENTERS OF THE FOOD. Each of them carries a platter of sliced turkey and stuffing, optional gravy and cranberry sauce, which will be served family style at the table.)

PRESENTERS OF THE FOOD

I'm now the server of the bird,
And blessed with Christmas cheer.
'Tis a delight, to have a bite,
And nice to have you here!

(PRESENTERS OF THE FOOD place their platters on the table and exit singing a verse from the song "HERE WE COME A-WASSAILING," accompanied by musicians)

PRESENTERS OF THE FOOD
(Singing to Here We come A-Wassailing)

Here we come a-wassailing
Among the leaves so green;
Here we come a-wand'ring
So fair to be seen.

REFRAIN:

Love and joy come to you,
And to you your wassail too;
And God bless you and send you a Happy New Year
And God send you a Happy New Year.

BRIEF INTERMISSION WHILE TURKEY COURSE IS SERVED AND EATEN

(MUSICIANS play a happy holiday song)

(PRESENTERS OF THE FOOD reappear during this time, to refresh the drinks. Backstage, the carafes have been refilled. After a suitable time, the scullery servants appear to remove the turkey platters and carafes. If any food remains on the platters or liquid remains in the carafes, they can ask, using a Cockney accent, *"Can I finish this up for ya, loves?"* At that point, they can place more food on the plates of those who want it and pour all remaining liquid into the glasses, of those who want to finish up. They then remove carafes.)

Act II, Scene 4

(The cheery holiday music of intermission now becomes somber. This signals the entrance of the GHOSTS OF CHRISTMAS YET TO COME. The GHOSTS slowly enter, taking their places, each at the center of three tables.)

GHOSTS OF CHRISTMAS YET TO COME

I am the ghost of what will be,
But only if you dare,
To frown your way through Christmas
And offer not a care

(Pause--mood changes--ghosts begin to smile as they produce sprigs of holly from their pockets. There should be one sprig for each person at the table.)

But if you offer many smiles
And to each a holly spring,
The ones who follow after me,
Will give you all...some pig!

(GHOSTS OF CHRISTMAS YET TO COME exit, singing a verse from the song, "ANGELS WE HAVE HEARD ON HIGH," accompanied by musicians.)

GHOSTS OF CHRISTMAS YET TO COME
(Singing "Angels We Have Heard on High")

Angels we have heard on high
Sweetly singing o'er the plain
And the mountains in reply
Echoing their joyous strains
Gloria, in excelsis Deo!
Gloria, in excelsis Deo!

Shepherds, why this jubilee?
Why your joyous strains prolong?
What the gladsome tidings be?
Which inspire your heavenly songs?

(PRESENTERS OF THE FOOD enter, each carrying a platter of sliced pork, a green vegetable and optional sauce/gravy.)

PRESENTERS OF THE FOOD

As you can see, this is a pig,
And we've been sent to say,
This Christmas dish may help you make
A Happy Holiday!

(PRESENTERS OF THE FOOD exit, while singing a slightly twisted verse from the song "THE TWELVE DAYS OF CHRISTMAS." MUSICIANS accompany them.)

PRESENTERS OF THE FOOD

(Singing the following of the song to the tune of ""The Twelve Days of Christmas" is an English Christmas carol)

On the First day of Christmas, my true love sent to me…
A Porker in a Pear Tree.

On the Second day of Christmas, my true love sent to me…
Two Turtle Doves
And a Porker in a Pear Tree.

On the Third day of Christmas, my true love sent to me…
Three French Hens,
Two Turtle Doves
And a Porker in a Pear Tree.

BRIEF INTERMISSION WHILE PORK COURSE IS PASSED AND EATEN

(MUSICIANS play a happy holiday song)

(After a suitable time, the SCULLERY SERVANTS appear. They remove the pork platters. If any food remains on the platters they can again ask, with a Cockney accent, again something like *"All done love, or would ya like the rest?"* At that point, they can place more food on the plates of those who want it. They then clear away the platters this time, they will also remove the dinner plates of those who are finished eating.)

ACT III

Scene 1

(The PRESENTERS OF THE FOOD enter, taking their regular places. Each is carrying a tray upon which is a large clear glass or plastic bowl of the traditional English dessert, trifle. They also carry dishes for the dessert. [Note: There are many variations of trifle. The dessert is--at its most basic--layers of fruit, cake and custard, sometimes topped with whipped cream.])

PRESENTERS OF THE FOOD

On Christmas day, we've all been known
To eat until we hurt.
But still, we hope you've made the room,
For an Englishman's dessert!

(At this point in the performance, they place the bowl and dessert plates on the table. They also finish removing any empty dinner plates. The PRESENTERS OF THE FOOD then begin to sing an adapted verse from the song, "WE WISH YOU A MERRY CHRISTMAS.")

PRESENTERS OF THE FOOD

(Singing to the song, "We Wish You a Merry Trifle")

We wish you a merry trifle,
We wish you a merry trifle,
We wish you a merry trifle,
And a Happy New Year!

(As they are singing, the rest of the company begins to enter the room and joins in the song as the lyrics change to the traditional words. The cast enters in order of appearance all singing.)

Good tidings we bring
To you and your kin;
We wish you a merry Christmas
And a happy New Year!

Oh, bring us some figgy pudding,
Oh, bring us some figgy pudding,
Oh, bring us some figgy pudding,
And bring it right here.

We won't go until we get some,
We won't go until we get some,
We won't go until we get some,
So bring it right here.

Good tidings we bring
To you and your kin;
We wish you a merry Christmas
And a happy New Year!

(The music begins to slow, signaling the last verse as a drawn out finale.)

We wish you…a merry Christmas
And a happy…New…Year!

(The company begins its curtain call, each group bowing separately and exiting following its applause. First, the COURT HERALDS step forward, bow and exit, then the QUEEN AND HER COURTIERS, followed by GHOSTS, TINY TIMS, SCROOGES, THE COMPANY OF ENTERTAINERS (MAGICIANS, ETC.), the SCULLERY SERVANTS and finally, the PRESENTERS OF THE FOOD. After all have exited, The Scrooge(s) re-enter and stand center stage where the audience can see them. They begin to speak.)

EBENEZER SCROOGE(S)

Just one more thought
To end this meal
Before we say "Good day,"

We have to thank
The blokes and birds
Who also made this play

The cooks we know
Worked long and hard
And we hope you liked their fare

(The cooks enter and stand behind Scrooge[s])

The musicians' art was
Well-rehearsed, so
To none can we compare

(Scrooge(s) point to the musicians and they all stand)

But there were those
Without whose jobs
Our words would have no flair

To our leaders in this stage event
Thanks much

For *being* there!

(SCROOGE(S) invite the DIRECTORS, PRODUCERS, COSTUMERS AND ALL OTHER BACKSTAGE WORKERS to enter onto the stage, as SCROOGE(S) and all others applaud. Before the applause dies down, they all bow and exit.)

THE END

END NOTES

END NOTES

END NOTES

END NOTES

END NOTES

END NOTES

www.ingramcontent.com/pod-product-compliance
Lightning Source LLC
Chambersburg PA
CBHW061311040426
42444CB00010B/2594